Molly's Parade

Mary Ebrecht

Illustrated by

Amazing Things Press

Illustrations by Tenna Hazen
Book design by Julie L. Casey

This book is a work of fiction. Any names, characters, or incidents are the product of the author's imagination and are used fictitiously. Any resemblance to actual events, locales, or persons, living or dead is purely coincidental.

ISBN 978-0692469132

Printed in the United States of America.

For more information, visit
WWW.AMAZINGTHINGSPRESS.COM

To Molly

Thanks for the memories.

To Blake
Grandma
Joe

Chapter One

The older white car pulled away from the stop sign and headed south. The driver knew where he was going. The voice on the phone had given clear directions. Three miles out of the small town, he recognized the landmark he had been told about. He knew it wouldn't be far now. The man at the wheel began to slow down the car as he rounded a bend in the road. Turning on his right turn signal, he pulled over on the shoulder and looked to the west. There she was. Leaning over slowly, he opened the glove box to lift out the binoculars. He brought them up to his face and focused them in her direction. Reaching for his cell phone, he hit speed dial 1, a number he knew well. A voice answered on the first ring. "Okay, I can see her. Do I go ahead and do it?" the man asked.

"No, you will know when. Just watch."

The man didn't have to wait long. "Okay, okay there she goes!" he said excitedly.

"You know what you have to do."

The man's hand went for the video camera. He couldn't believe it. This was going to make news!

The couple sitting on their porch swing looked at each other. Yep, there was another newcomer to the area, just waiting for Molly to do her stuff. They continued to watch as the short, balding man got out of his car to film their donkey. Sara smiled. "You were right, Tom. This is the third one this week."

They chuckled as the man began filming their donkey, Molly. The donkey could be seen coming up the hill with a menagerie of animals to start her parade. She still enjoyed performing for folks who stopped along the blacktop to watch her. As she and her followers got to the fence line near the observer, Molly began her parade. Behind her in order were Indie, a horse, followed by two cows, and two corgis. What a sight!

The animals paraded back and forth for their audience of one before they broke the formation and went in their own directions, except for Molly and Indie. They were always together.

Coming from around the corner of the house were Tom and Sara's two children, Jacob and Jessica. "Dad, Mom!" they said in unison. "How many does that make now?"

Tom laughed and replied, "I have lost count, kids."

Jumping up and down, blue-eyed Jessica begged, "Please tell us the story again."

"Why what story is that?" Sara teased.

"You know, Momma, the one about Molly. How you went and got her and Daddy had to chase her and he fell down and...."

"Hold on kiddo," Tom interrupted. "Do you want to tell the story or let Mommy?"

"Mommy, Mommy!" they both cried enthusiastically.

"Start at the very beginning, Mom," Jacob pleaded. "We want to hear it all."

Sara had told this story so many times. The

children knew it by heart but still loved to hear how they came to have Molly and how she had entertained them with her antics.

Chapter Two

Sara took a deep breath and began the story. "Late one summer 12 years ago, a friend of mine told me about a donkey her aunt wanted to give away...."

"Give away?" squealed Sara.

"Why don't you go see her and then decide?" her friend laughed. She knew Sara loved animals and was sure to take the donkey.

That night Sara spoke to her husband of eight months about the free donkey. He reluctantly agreed to go look at the donkey.

Two days later, Tom and Sara pulled up in the gravel drive in their old rusty truck, pulling a small horse trailer behind them. The worn tires made a crunching noise as they rolled over the small rocks.

All of a sudden, they heard a gawd-awful noise that made them both think they had just run over a small animal. Tom quickly put the old truck in park and they both jumped out to see what had been squashed on the road. They heard it again. UH HUH! UH HUH! Turning toward the sound, they heard HEE HAW HEE HAW! It was a donkey with its long ears laid back and its mouth wide open. Molly the donkey was a great guard "dog" and she was letting her owner, Aunt Gail, know there were strangers in the yard.

The screen door of the old yellow house slammed shut as Aunt Gail came out to greet Tom and Sara. "What a gorgeous morning," she said as she reached out to shake hands with the couple. "My name is Gail Penders, and you must be Tom and Sara."

"Good morning," Tom and Sara replied.

Gail thought they seemed like such a nice couple. She felt sure Molly would have a good home.

"What can you tell us about your donkey?" Tom asked as he put his arm around Sara's shoulders.

"Well," began Gail, "you saw what a good guard dog she is. Molly is also a leader and is affectionate when she gets to know you. She does get stubborn now and then, but that is normal for a donkey. She can be strong willed and has a mind of her own."

"Has that been a problem for you?" questioned Tom.

"Not really. Once in awhile, Molly and I don't agree, but she hasn't shown that side of herself in quite some time."

"So why are you wanting to give this donkey away?" Tom asked cautiously.

"I am just getting too old to take care of her anymore," she replied sadly.

Tom looked at his wife who was pleading with

her eyes. He knew they would be taking the donkey home. "Of course, we'll take her." Tom felt a twinge in his stomach but he chose to ignore it. Sara clapped her hands and squealed with delight. She couldn't wait to get her donkey home.

Over the next hour, Sara and Gail sat under the ancient oak tree, sipping ice-cold lemonade, and watched Tom try to persuade Molly to get in the trailer.

He slowly came around to the front of his truck. Sweat trickled down his forehead and into his eyes. Tom wiped the mud from his arms and shirt with his handkerchief and stared at the old woman. Gail just smiled and shrugged her shoulders. That donkey had given him a merry chase around the pen and into the pig lot. Molly had made a real game of playing tag with Tom but he saw no humor in it. He was exhausted.

Later, Tom swore that donkey had pushed him

into that pigpen. "And look at her now," grumbled Tom under his breath. "She's quietly munching on the oats we brought for her to eat on the way home. Well, at least she is in the trailer," thought Tom as he slowly got into his truck.

Sara and Gail arose from their lawn chairs. They had been witness to the battle of wills between man and beast while they sipped cold lemonade and enjoyed the cool breeze that passed their way.

After goodbyes were said, Tom and Sara pulled out onto the highway and headed for home. A mile or so down the road, Sara spoke up and told Tom how sorry she was that Molly had been so stubborn about climbing into the trailer. Tom smiled weakly but thought to himself about how he would like to get even with that cantankerous donkey. You just wait, he thought. I'll show that animal who's boss!

During the ride home, Molly continued to eat her oats and watch the scenery pass by. She was giving some thought about her new owners. What an amusing pastime they would be for her. She reflected on this as the trailer bounced behind the truck to its final destination.

Chapter Three

After arriving home, Tom continued down to the opened gate where Molly could step down into the pasture that was to be her home. It sounded easy...but it wasn't. The donkey just looked at Tom and Sara while her long ears moved back and forth.

Tom and Sara just stood there speechless. Molly would not get out of the trailer! Slapping her hindquarter was no help either. Molly's legs were stiff as boards and she wasn't budging.

"How are we going to get her out?" Sara asked worriedly. Tom smiled. "I know what will get that donkey moving." He pulled the trailer forward. He unhooked the pickup and drove through the gate, backing the old truck up until it was close to the trailer. Jumping out of the truck, Tom grabbed a long piece of sturdy rope from the bed, tied one end firmly to the hitch and slipped the other end over Molly's head before she realized what he had done.

Whispering to the donkey Tom gloated, "Now, donkey, we will see who wins this round." As he put the truck in drive and began moving forward slowly, Molly's eyes grew big and her ears laid back. She dug her hooves in and locked her knees. She would not go easily. Pushing the accelerator down a little more, Tom felt a little give in the rope. Looking back, Tom saw that the darn donkey's neck was stretched as far as it would go, but she hadn't moved at all. Tom's foot once again pushed down on the accelerator, giving it a bit more gas. Molly began to move, but she came out braying and bucking all the way.

Making his way cautiously to the pig-headed donkey, he swore he saw a smile on her lips. Then she turned until he could see a full view of her backside and then walked away. Sara tried hard not to laugh but didn't succeed.

Over the next few days Sara would come out every morning and brush Molly and talk to her. Molly didn't know what she was saying but she liked the sound of her voice. When she was done, Sara would give Molly two apples, which turned out to be her favorite. It would also get her in trouble.

One morning Sara did not come out. Molly decided to look for some juicy red apples herself. Walking along the fence, she kept her nose up sniffing for sweet apples she had come to expect every morning from Sara.

As she came near the end of the fence line that separated the pasture from the adjoining farm, her nose started twitching. Molly knew she was close. Over the fence she jumped, running for the apples she now saw at the edge of the neighbor's yard.

Sara got a call about 20 minutes later. It was their neighbor to the north. "Did you and Tom get a donkey?" the neighbor asked.

"Yes we did. Why? Have you seen her?" Sara closed her eyes. She knew what the next words would be.

"Well, your donkey has taken a liking to our apples. And you know my wife likes to make pies from them."

"Yes, I know she enjoys baking."

"Well then, could you keep that donkey at your place? I don't know what my wife is capable of if she sees that donkey getting in to her apples." Sara sighed and promised to come right away and get Molly.

Once more, Sara began feeding Molly apples and brushing her coat every day. Only one day she was very busy in the house and did not have time to bring Molly her two apples. Sara was washing dishes *and when she looked up, there was Molly pushing her nose against the window! She wanted her two apples. Tom never figured out how she got out.*

Once on a warm sunny day in June, Sara was out back hanging clothes out to dry. With no warning at all, Sara heard a familiar gawd-awful sound. UH HUH! UH HUH, and then HEE HAW, HEE HAW. Sara went running to the pasture. There was Molly, up by fence line that was closest to the highway. She was standing there, each ear going back and forth. Far in the distance, Sara heard a high-pitched siren, then a lower pitched siren. Within a short time, a fire truck went speeding by with an ambulance right behind it. After all the noise had settled, so did Molly. Sara just laughed and shook her head. She marveled at the number of things Molly could do.

Chapter Four

One night Tom told Sara his Uncle Bob had asked if they would adopt his old horse Indie. It took very little time to come to a decision. Molly was going to have a friend.

Getting Indie into and out of the trailer was easy. She was so well mannered and they were glad they brought her home.

They weren't the only ones who were glad to have the old horse; so was Molly. It seemed the old horse and ornery donkey became friends on sight. From then on, wherever you saw one, the other was there too. The only strange thing about it, when the two walked, Molly always led, never Indie. Indie didn't seem to mind though.

One hot afternoon, Sara was sitting on the porch

when she noticed a car had pulled over and was watching Molly.

"Well I'll be!" she thought to herself. Not only was Indie behind her but the cow was, too!

From that day on, Sara would often see a car or truck pull off the highway to watch the animals perform. "It was like watching a parade," giggled Sara when she told Tom.

The word soon got out that there was a donkey leading a parade of animals on a farm in Wells

County. After that, traffic would get pretty heavy on some days. Everyone was curious about the donkey's parade.

A news reporter from the neighboring county came and interviewed Tom and Sara. After that story ran in the paper, cars would be backed up on the highway trying to get a peek at Molly's parade.

Although Tom didn't know exactly when, one day he noticed Molly was no longer performing. She did not form her parade for a long time. No one ever knew why.

After two years, Tom and Sara decided they would like to add a baby to their family. Jacob would be that baby.

When Sara was carrying Jacob in her tummy, Molly's behavior changed. Sara would come out to brush and feed her as usual, but Molly did something she had not done before. She began *nibbling on Sara's shirt, not to eat it, but just to put the top between her lips. Molly then would rub her head against Sara's tummy!*

Jessica interrupted, "Mommy tell what Molly did when I was in your tummy."

Sara smiled and ruffled her daughter's soft, brown hair. "Okay kiddo, I was just coming to that."

Now things were different when Sara was carrying Jessica. Sara noticed Molly would sometimes ignore her when she called for her to come for her daily brushing and have her two apples. One day when Sara saw Molly in a small pen near the house, she decided to brush and feed her right there. Unexpectedly, Molly whirled around, laid her ears back, and bared her teeth.

Charging right at Sara, Molly nearly hit her. Luckily Sara was close to the gate and got out, locking it just as Molly put on her brakes to keep her head from hitting the gate. Sara did not attempt to feed her until after baby Jessica was born.

When Sara would call for Molly after Jessica's birth, that ornery donkey was back to her normal self. Tom spoke to the vet about the change in her disposition, but the vet just shook his head. He could not explain this odd behavior. Tom and Sara decided it was just one of Molly's quirks.

At this point in the story, Tom spoke up and said, "I think it is time for Jacob and me to tell some of our experiences with Molly."

"Yeah Dad," added Jacob. "Tell about how she decided she liked you."

Tom began...

The first winter with the family, Molly would watch Tom closely as he would bring out hay for her,

Indie, and the two cows. She also observed how he would break up the ice in the winter so they could get to the water in the special tank that was just for Molly and her friends. Soon Tom noticed she was not as ornery as usual. She had accepted him as her friend. Tom was sure glad that once ornery donkey was not going to misbehave anymore. Sara would always be Molly's favorite though.

One Sunday when the family had just returned from church, they heard the donkey braying. Jacob recognized right away the braying sounded different than the one she used when the ambulance or fire truck went by. At once he told his father. Quickly they headed for the area of pasture they thought Molly was calling from. There before them was one of the cows with a new bull calf and Molly standing over them like a protective mother. The calf was not supposed to be born for two more weeks. Molly saved them both by letting the family know about the early arrival.

Molly became protective of the little calf for a couple of months. The young cow accepted Molly and allowed her to stay close to her baby.

The most recent experience with Molly was their

favorite of the stories. This story included this same young cow and her calf. During supper one evening, Tom noticed Molly up near the edge of the fence line closest to the yard. She was pacing back and forth making those sounds that he knew was going to turn into a loud Hee-Haw! Hee Haw!

Once Molly saw Tom and Jacob coming, she turned and trotted toward the pond, never looking back. When they got there they saw why Molly had raised such a fuss. Both cow and calf were stuck in the mud that was at the bottom of the pond.

Luckily both were close to the edge. Tom and Jacob knew what they had to. Tom ran for the pickup while Jacob stayed and tried to keep mother and baby calm. After pulling the calf out together, they placed a rope around the cow's neck and pulled her out with the truck. Molly had saved their lives. Molly was rewarded with two ears of juicy yellow corn from the garden.

Two things happened about the same time one fall. Sara and Tom bought a corgi for each of the children. Jacob and Jessica loved them. Molly didn't.

When the dogs would come out in the pasture, Molly would chase them under the fence if she was close enough. Taco and Sassy soon learned their place. If Molly's parade started up, they knew to stay in the back. If they didn't, Molly would remind them. Once in a while, some people would swear they saw a donkey followed by a horse, cow and calf, with two dogs bringing up the rear.

Another thing that happened that fall was when Tom and Sara noticed something different about

Indie. She walked almost up against Molly. In turn, Molly walked slower too. They also noted when Molly was not near the old horse, Indie would begin to whinny until Molly was with her again. The old horse was blind and Molly had become her caregiver. This donkey really loved her old friend.

As Tom ended his stories, Sara stood up. She always got teary eyed with that part of the story; besides, supper needed to be fixed. Tom stood and stretched. The chores wouldn't do themselves. He left the children still sitting there, watching the animals.

"Look!" Jessica laughed. Jacob smiled. Out on the highway a red van slowed and pulled over onto the side of the road. A family got out and walked to the fence.

Jacob and Jessica could hear the children's voices in the quiet of the evening. "Look Mommy and

Daddy!" Molly and her friends headed to the top of

the hill to begin their parade.

The End

ACKNOWLEDGEMENTS

It is clear the author who writes the story is only a piece of the whole that makes a story possible.

My thanks go out to the following:

Molly, who happens to be a real donkey. This wonderful story is based on her and her other animal friends.

My Family: You were honest with me when editing my manuscript.

Jason Offutt: Your writing class gave me a good knowledge base to begin my new adventure. Also, after editing my final draft the words you wrote inspired me, "You need to get this published."

My sweet husband Bob: You pestered me for years to write my stories down that I told our grandchildren when they were small. You felt I should share them with other children so they could enjoy them also.

Amazing Things Press: You took a chance on me. Thank You just doesn't seem to cover it.

Above all else, I want to thank the Lord for all the blessings he rains down on me every day. Without Him, there would be nothing.

ABOUT THE AUTHOR:

Mary resides in Maryville, Mo with her husband Bob. She has worked in healthcare for the past 41 years. They have two grown children, Greg and Debra. Craig and Lily are the perfect grandchildren. It doesn't get any better than that! After several years of encouragement from Bob, Mary tried her hand at writing. Her first children's book is Molly's Parade. Mary works full time, plays with her grandchildren, goes camping, and is currently working on a poetry book and another children's book.

For more information, please go to:
www.maryebrecht.weebly.com.

A MESSAGE FROM THE AUTHOR:

Thank you for taking the time to read my book. I would be honored if you would consider leaving a review for it on **Amazon**.

ABOUT THE ILLUSTRATOR:

Tenna Hazen graduated with a Bachelors of Fine Arts from Northwest Missouri State University. She resides in Maryville, Missouri with her husband and three children. She enjoys painting, drawing, watercolors, jewelry making, refinishing furniture and crafting. Her Facebook page is called By Tenna, from which she sells many of her treasures.

Check out these titles from
Amazing Things Press

Keeper of the Mountain by Nshan Erganian

Rare Blood Sect by Robert L. Justus

Evolving by James Fly

Survival In the Kitchen by Sharon Boyle

Stop Beating the Dead Horse by Julie L. Casey

In Daddy's Hands by Julie L. Casey

How I Became a Teenage Survivalist by Julie L. Casey

Time Lost: Teenage Survivalist II by Julie L. Casey

Starlings by Jeff Foster

MariKay's Rainbow by Marilyn Weimer

Convolutions by Vashti Daise

Seeking the Green Flash by Lanny Daise

Nikki's Heart by Nona j. Moss

Nightmares or Memories by Nona j. Moss

Thought Control by Robert L. Justus

Palightte by James Fly

I, Eugenius by Larry W. Anderson

Tales From Beneath the Crypt by Megan Marie

Vintage Mysteries by Megan Marie

Defenders of Holt by Julie L. Casey

A Thin Strip of Green by Vashti Daise

Fun Activities to Help Little Ones Talk by Kathy Blair

Trade of the Tricks: The Tricks' Brand by David Noe

Tears and Prayers by Harold W. "Doc" Arnett

Thoughts of Mine by Thomas Kirschner

Pass of the Crow by Whitney Grady

Bighorn by James Ozenberger

Check out these children's titles from
Amazing Things Press

The Boy Who Loved the Sky by Donna E. Hart
Terreben by Donna E. Hart
Sherry Strawberry's Clubhouse by Donna E. Hart
Finally Fall by Donna E. Hart
Thankful for Thanksgiving by Donna E. Hart
Make Room for Maggie by Donna E. Hart
Toddler Tales by Kathy Blair
A Cat Named Phyl by Donna E. Hart
Geography Studies With Animal Buddies by Vashti Daise
The Princess and the Pink Dragon by Thomas Kirschner
Sherry Strawberry's Coloring & Activity Book by Donna E. Hart
The Happy Butterfly by Donna E. Hart
From Seanna by Vashti Daise
The Boy Who Had Nine Cats by Irene Alexander
Meet Mr. Wiggles by Shivonne Jean Hancock
From Seanna Coloring Book by Vashti Daise
The Special Letter Day by Cyndee Veale
True Heart by Irene Alexander
A Cat, a Pig, and the Boys by Thomas Kirschner

Amazing Things Press

www.amazingthingspress.com

Made in the USA
San Bernardino, CA
14 September 2015